History Detective 1

Bruce Jamieson

Oliver & Boyd

Contents

Oliver & Boyd
Robert Stevenson House
1-3 Baxter's Place
Leith Walk
Edinburgh EH1 3BB

A Division of Longman Group UK Ltd

First published 1985
Sixth Impression 1986

Set in 12pt Monophoto Gill Sans and Times New Roman

Produced by Longman Group (FE) Limited
Printed in Hong Kong

ISBN 0-05-003646-7

Acknowledgments

The author and publishers are grateful to those listed below for permission to reproduce the following:
Ron Bowen © The Rainbird Publishing Group, artwork: 10 (reproduced with permission from *The Making of Mankind* by Richard Leakey); Trustees of the British Museum, photographs: 12(4, bottom), 15(left), 16, 20(left), 26; British Society for the Turin Shroud, photograph: 17(left); Curtis Brown Ltd, London for extracts from *The Tomb of Tutankhamun* by Howard Carter; Edinburgh City Libraries (I F Grant Collection) photograph: 38; Faber and Faber Publishers for extracts from a Tacitus translation and photographs: 5, 6, 7, 8 all from *The Bog People* by P V Glob published by them; Mr A. G. Gordon, Haddo House, map: 37 (Scottish Record Office RHP. 9942); Griffith Institute, Ashmolean Museum, photographs: 22, 23, 24, 25 (top and bottom), 27 (2); Robert Harding Picture Library, cover photo; Mansell Collection, photograph: 18; Mary Rose Trust, photograph: 31; Trustees of the National Library of Scotland, illustrations: 13, 14, 15 (right); National Museum of the Antiquities of Scotland, photographs: cover, 39; Portsmouth City Museums and Art Galleries, illustration: 29; The Royal Scottish Museum, photograph: 12 (top); Weidenfeld & Nicolson Ltd, photographs: 17 (2, right, by Yigael Yadin); Betty Wilsher, photographs: 40 and 41 (6).
Other photographs are from the author's private collection.

Illustrated by Alistair Stewart (page 34 map), Pat Tourret and Ken Wilson

1. A Murder Mystery

You are a police detective called in to investigate this murder after a neighbour has reported seeing broken glass on the front lawn.

1. *How do you act on entering the room? Why must you be careful?*
2. *What interesting and important things can you see?*
3. *What help do these give you:*
   (a) the broken window;
   (b) the footprint;
   (c) the empty glasses;
   (d) the clocks;
   (e) the poker;
   (f) the unopened handbag?
4. *Which of these clues might help you to say:*
   (a) When the crime was commited;
   (b) Whether the murderer was male or female;
   (c) what was the murder weapon;
   (d) whether the murderer knew his victim?
5. *What else would you do:*
   (a) in the room;
   (b) in the neighbourhood;
   (c) at Headquarters?
6. *Do you know who the murderer is or is your information not yet complete?*
7. *Write out what you do know about the criminal.*
8. *How have you found out this information?*

9. *Have you just been guessing? If not what part have these played in your enquiry: experience; previous knowledge; techniques of finding out; methods of procedure?*
10. *Nobody actually saw the crime. Why is that a disadvantage?*

However there is one witness, the neighbour.

Oh there was a terrible noise last night – shouting and crashing, something terrible. She's usually such a quiet girl too. Out most nights she is . . . I mean 'was'. . . . Oh it's terrible. What will the papers make of it?... I was just saying to my Eddie. . . .

1. *Is the witness male or female, reliable and helpful?*
2. *Does the statement fit in with what you know?*

It is proved that the murder weapon was a hard, straight object.

The film in the camera reveals several pictures of the same man.

The letter on the table reads:

Dear Elizabeth Tuesday 24th April
I must see you. Don't say 'no' again. I'll be round Thursday on my night off. Be there.
Richard.

1. *How would you describe the tone of the letter?*
2. *Is there evidence that the writer was "our man"?*

Richard is arrested. His fingerprints and footprint match those in the murder room.

1. *Offer a likely explanation of the events on the evening of the 26th. List the clues you collected under these headings:*
   (a) written evidence
   (b) oral [spoken] evidence
   (c) picture evidence
   (d) object evidence
   (e) dating evidence
   (f) tell-tale marks

A police detective looks for such clues for a very special purpose.

1. *What is he trying to do?*

A history detective also gathers evidence after an event has taken place. Many of his methods are similar to those of the crime detector but his aims are different.

1. *Why does a history detective gather evidence?*

Let us be history detectives and investigate another mystery.

2. The Grauballe Murder Enquiry

Saturday, 26 April 1952
Nebelgard Fen near the town of Grauballe, Denmark.
Some peat-cutters have shouted out and shown you what they have uncovered. Sticking out from the ground is a dark-coloured human head with a stubbly chin, short-cropped, red-brown hair and dark eyes. The face, squashed by the weight of the peat, is twisted into a look of fear. Looking closer you see a long deep cut round the front of the neck, from ear to ear. The man has been murdered!
After further digging the naked body measuring five feet four inches [164 cm] is fully exposed, and taken for examination to Police HQ at Aarhus.

The man suffered from rheumatoid arthritis — a disease that usually starts at 30. The condition of the teeth confirms that age, and their worn state suggests that the man ate plenty of meat.

The hands are smooth and unused to rough work. There are no records of the fingerprints.

The stomach contents reveal that his last meal was a soup made up of sixty ingredients including buttercup, yarrow, clover, rye, dockin and barley.

1. *Write a description of this mystery man for circulation to a newspaper.*

In response an old farmer's-wife comes forward:

The man was a peat-cutter called Christian. He disappeared without trace about 65 years ago. Yes, that's him all right. He was stooped with consumption and he drank you know. He must have fallen into the bog . . . and drowned.

The first picture of Grauballe man

1. *Explain whether or not you believe this evidence.*

The police are not convinced and decide to seek advice from other experts. They call in the history detectives who do not come unprepared, as other bodies have been found in similar circumstances. After studying the pollen-grains in the peat surrounding the body, the history detectives make a startling announcement. The earth around the body dates from the time of Christ's birth.

1. *How long ago was that?*

Another test measures the amount of radio-active carbon in the body. Every living thing contains this but after death the amount gradually decreases. By measuring how much is left in body-tissue it is possible to calculate its age. By this method our 'Grauballe man' is proved to be 1650 years old!

No wonder the police in Aarhus had no fingerprint record. They were looking at some of the oldest hands ever seen. Their owner had lived in the Iron Age and had been preserved by natural minerals in the peat.

The police now knew that they were not dealing with a recent murder but the history detectives were still curious.

About 160 similar corpses had been unearthed and in every case the body had been strangled, beheaded or mutilated.

1. *Why had no one reported anything suspicious?*

One man, however, had left written evidence from the past. He was Tacitus, a Roman who wrote in 100 AD:

These people [of Denmark] worship the Goddess Nerthus, Mother Earth, and do not consider it fitting with the greatness of her heavenly powers to confine her within four walls or to represent her in the likeness of a human face. They make holy groves and give the name 'Goddess' to that secret presence which they can see only in awe and adoration.

Rough carving of the goddess Nerthus

Tacitus talks about the Goddess being worshipped as a "secret presence" — something "not understood". One thing that the Iron Age people would not understand would be the changing of the seasons: what made the sun get lower in the sky during winter and return again with better weather in spring. All they did know was that if Spring did not come and help their crops to grow then they would starve.

Worshipping an "unknown presence" like the coming of spring — pictured as a powerful Goddess — would be very important for these early people.

1. *What other name had Nerthus which would fit this theory?*
2. *Look at the photograph on page 6. How has the carving been made?*

We have discovered something interesting about the history detective. He is not only concerned with finding evidence in order to solve problems of the past. He must also take into account how people lived and what they believed in.

1. *Does our knowledge of Iron Age beliefs and attitudes help solve our murder mystery?*

Tacitus adds more information:

On an island in a holy grove is a holy chariot, covered in robes. Only one priest is permitted to touch it. He interprets the presence of the Goddess in her shrine and follows with deep reverence as she rides away drawn by oxen. Then come days of rejoicing and all places keep holyday. Every weapon is put away. Peace and quiet are alone known until the priest returns the Goddess to her temple when she has had her fill of the society of mortals. After this the chariot, robes and the goddess herself are washed in a secret pool. Slaves are the holy servants and afterwards they are straightaway killed and put in the same pool.

1. *What signs might the priest 'interpret' to suggest that Nerthus was ready for her spring journey (ie that spring had begun)?*
2. *What must happen at that time?*
3. *Why were the slaves killed?*
4. *What do you think the carving below was meant to show?*

A human sacrifice to the Earth Goddess — let us see whether the death of Grauballe Man fits this theory.

Perhaps the best clue is the newly-eaten food in his stomach.

1. *Were there any summer or autumn fruits in the list?*
2. *With what season were the seeds connected?*
3. *How do you know that Grauballe man did not usually eat seeds?*

This peculiar carving was found near a bog burial

It seems likely that before being sacrificed he ate a special ceremonial gruel, containing those crops which Nerthus was to make grow.

In 1954 this ritual soup was made on television to the 2000-year-old-recipe. It was tasted by Sir Mortimer Wheeler, a famous history detective. He said:

I shall need to wash it down with some good Danish brandy. It would have been punishment enough for Grauballe Man to have been forced to eat this gruel for the rest of his life, however terrible his crime might have been.

1. *Did Sir Mortimer like the gruel?*
2. *Does this suggest it was typical food for Iron Age men?*
3. *What else made it special?*
4. *For what reason did Sir Mortimer imply the man died?*

Here is another problem of being a history detective. Whatever conclusion may be reached about the past, the best that can usually be said is that it is **probably** true.

The bog-man might have been killed as a punishment for a crime. However, when we look at our evidence and include these objects found in other similar deaths then our "sacrifice" theory looks good.

Symbolic neck rings of the goddess Nerthus

Who exactly was Grauballe man?

Although history detection concerns finding out about people we do not always know their names.

1. *What do we know about the unknown body?*
   Were his hands those of a working slave?
2. *Why was he chosen to perform the cleaning-ceremony and be sacrificed?*

This evidence from Tacitus will help:

A branch cut from a fruit-bearing tree is divided into small splinters each marked with a distinctive sign so that it can be distinguished from the others.

1. *Is this a fair method of choosing?*
2. *What is your opinion of human sacrifices?*

In order to have opinions about people who lived in the past it is necessary to gather a great deal of evidence. The collection of such clues requires a great deal of effort and skill.

1. *The investigation of Grauballe Man made use of many different kinds of evidence. What use was made of:*
   (a) eye-witnesses;
   (b) written evidence;
   (c) discovered objects;
   (d) previous knowledge from other investigations?
2. *What other kinds of evidence were gathered?*
3. *What kind of training does a history detective require?*

3. The Trouble with Time

The peat-cutters of Grauballe were out in their time-scale. They thought they had found a recent crime, but historical knowledge helped to prove that the murder was 2000 years old and had happened in time 'long-past'.

Let us see what the history detective means by 'past'. It can mean 'yesterday' or 'many years ago', but we must find an accurate way of measuring it.

1. *Copy out these time-measurements from the smallest to the largest:*

hour	year	minute	month
second	week	fortnight	day.

Some of these units of time are so small that you can remember what you were doing then.

1. *What were you doing one second ago, one hour ago, one day ago?*
2. *How would you define the word* day*?*
3. *What were you doing exactly one year ago?*

You will **not** remember what you were doing ten years ago, a period called a **decade**.

A Time Line

1. *Draw a line (like the one below) measuring 1 cm for every year of your life. Starting with the year of your birth, mark off the years up to the present.*

Below certain dates write any important events that have happened to you.

It is always important to arrange dates in the correct order. This accurate arrangement is called **chronology**. If you get the chronology right you will have drawn a correct time line which begins with the first decade of your life.

1. *Ten decades make up one* **century***. How many years is that?*
2. *Ten centuries make up a* **millenium** *(plural* **millenia***). How many years is that?*
3. *How many millenia ago did Grauballe Man live?*
4. *Guess how long ago the first man on Earth lived?*

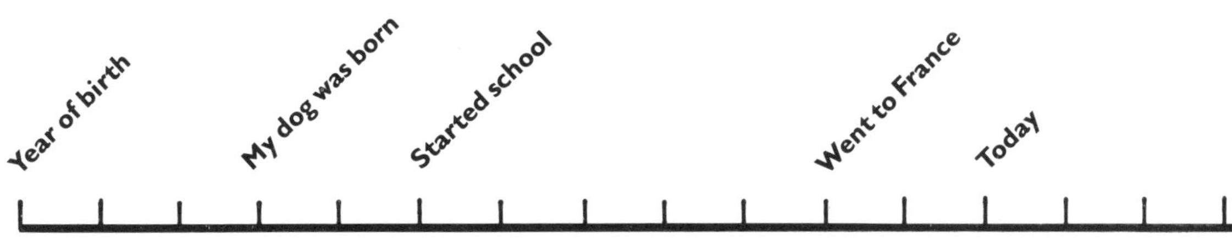

Time Line

The First Man?

One history detective who has been trying to answer this last question is Richard Leakey. In Africa he came across some extraordinary footprints.

Dr Leakey said:

They are the most remarkable find I ever made. When I came across them I must admit I was not sure but then it became clear that they could be . . . nothing else than the earliest prints of man's ancestors. They show us that hominids $3\frac{3}{4}$ million years ago walked upright with a free-striding gait just as we do today.

1. *What word does Leakey use for an early man-like creature?*
2. *What does he say the marks are?*

The proof of this claim comes from the fact that the ash in which the prints were made came from the volcano, Sadiman, and could only have been laid down 3¾ million years ago. A light rain made the ash perfect for taking prints and hot sunshine just afterwards turned the ash rock-hard, preserving for ever the marks upon it. More ash covered the tracks until their recent discovery. There, in the clay, is a record of life on earth 3750 millenia ago; 375000 decades into the past!

Large raindrops splashed onto the newly-fallen ash leaving tiny craters. The clouds passed; the promised downpour was yet to come. Various animals left their tracks in the damp ash: hares, guinea-fowl, elephants, rhinoceroses, hyaenas, a sabre-tooth tiger and baboons.

And so did three hominids. A large individual, probably a male, walked slowly towards the North. Following behind was a smaller individual who, for some reason, placed its feet in the prints of the first. A youngster skipped along by their side turning at one point to look to its left.

Leakey

1. *Recapture this moment in time by writing a story about the making of these tracks. (Look at the illustration below.)*

An artist's impression of these early hominids. They probably had no language but could only make grunting noises.

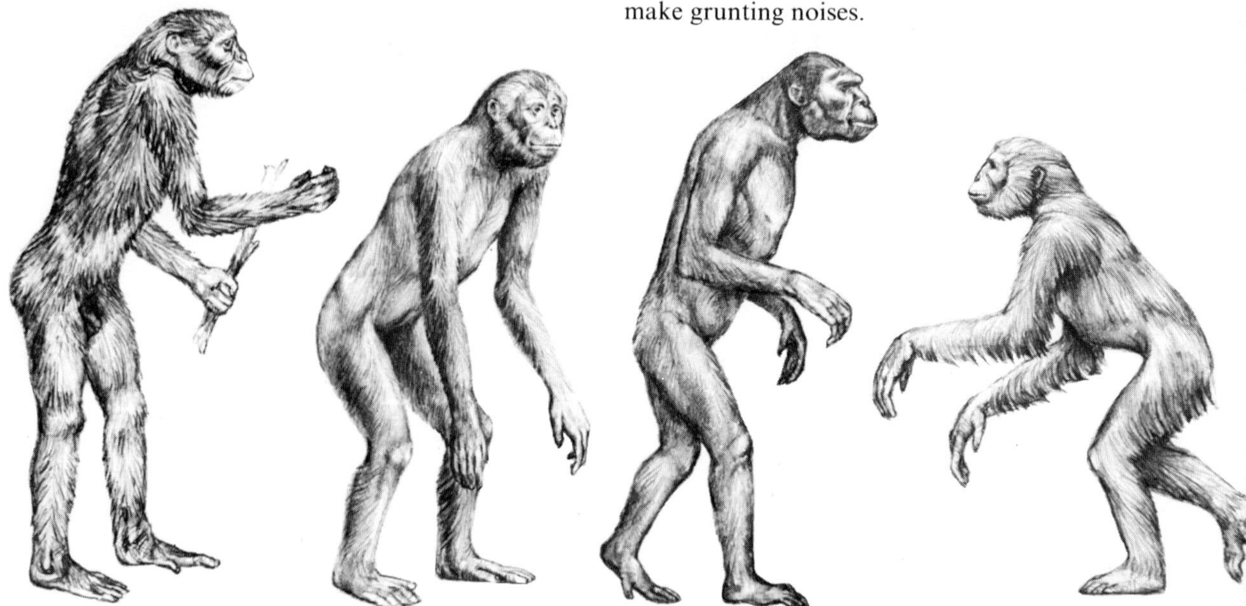

The Last Minute

It is very difficult to imagine life so long ago and yet, compared to the age of the world, it is not a long time. Imagine that the whole history of the world is represented by this twelve-hour clock, which started to tick at the moment the world 'began'.

After that came:

Ancient times: from 5000 years ago until 1500 years ago

Medieval times: from 1500 years ago until 500 years ago

Modern times: from 500 years ago until today.

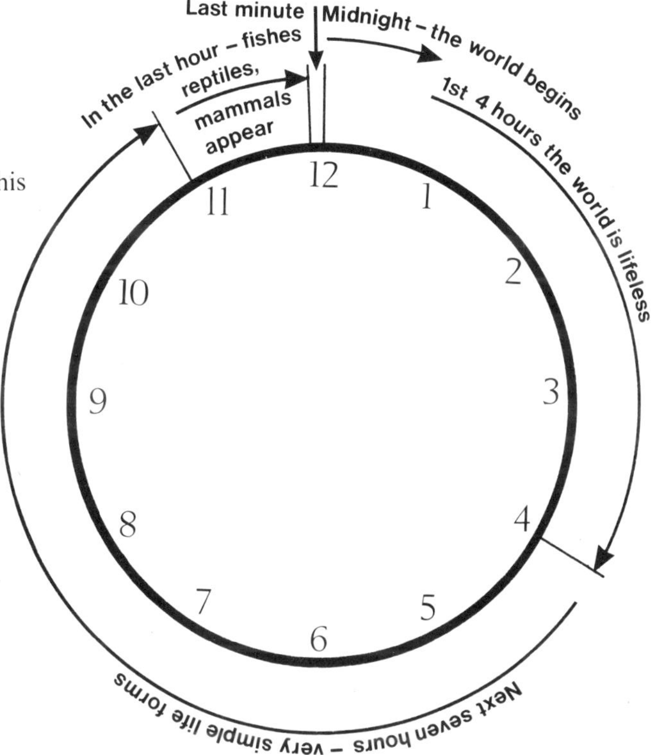

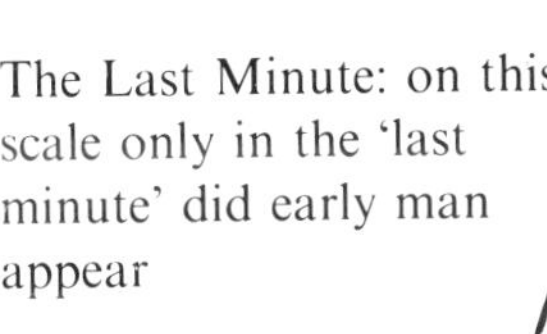
The Last Minute: on this scale only in the 'last minute' did early man appear

On this time-scale the history detective is really only interested in the last 'minute' of the past. That does not seem very long but an incredible amount has happened in the three million years which that 'minute' really represents.

In that time man developed from the simple ape-like creatures through several **ages** named after what objects were made from at that time: the **Stone Age**, the **Bronze Age** and the **Iron Age**. (You can read about them in *Ancient Britons* in the *Exploring History* series.)

A history detective studies the evidence left by mankind during this time. He is less interested in the period before man which we call **prehistoric** times: that is to say before 'history'.

Dating

In order to make more sense of this huge period of time, history detectives give dates to each year. This is especially useful for identifying the huge amount of evidence from more recent times.

1. What is today's date?

You have given today a day, a month and a year. The year you have chosen is the number of years since the birth of Jesus Christ. His birth in the year 1 is the starting-point for our dating system.

The first hundred years after the birth of Christ: the years 1-99 we call the first century A.D. (The letters stand for Anno Domini, in the year of our Lord.) The years A.D. 100 to A.D. 199 we call the second century A.D.

1. In which century are we living today?

Agricola became Roman Governor of Britain in A.D. 75, in the first century A.D.

1. In which century did:
the Vikings attack Lindisfarne (A.D. 900);
Vasco da Gama discover India (A.D. 1498);
Mary, Queen of Scots die (A.D. 1587);
Bonnie Prince Charlie arrive in Scotland (A.D. 1745);
World War Two start (A.D. 1939)?
(These, and many more dates can be found in the *Exploring History* series.)

2. In which century were each of these four coins made?

3. This coin was made for Alexander the Great who ruled 400 years before Jesus was born. How old is it?

Coin of Alexander the Great

If something happened before the birth of Christ we call that date B.C. In order to calculate how long ago a date B.C. was we have to add on the number of years since Christ's birth to the number of years before Christ was born.

1. In which century B.C. and how long ago was:
(a) the landing of Julius Caesar in Britain (55 B.C.);
(b) the building of the Great Pyramid of Egypt (2686 B.C.);
(c) the start of the Stone Age (8000 B.C.)?

Commonwealth Coin

Farthing

Britannia Groat

Cartwheel Twopence

4. The Early History Detectives

How do we know about times long past? Why should we want to know?

This is where the police detective and the history detective differ most. Both are concerned about events in past time, but a history detective is not interested in bringing anyone to justice. He wants to find out about the past for its own sake, and learn about what has gone before from the clues which he and others have discovered.

The further back we look the more difficult it is to find clues. We must look for help from many experts: palaeontologists, epigraphists, calligraphists, linguists, paleographers, numismatists.

1. *From a dictionary find out which of these is an expert on: coins, inscriptions, languages, manuscripts, handwriting, fossils?*

THE ILLUSTRATED LONDON NEWS

Saturday, February 3, 1863

In the British Museum an exhibition has been opened to the public of a collection of classic marbles from Asia Minor made by the celebrated traveller and discoverer-of-the past: the Archaeologist Charles Fellowes and brought to this country at government expense.

Another expert who provides valuable information is the **archaeologist**.

1. *Read the notice above right:*
   - (a) *Why had Mr Fellowes visited the Ancient World;*
   - (b) *What does the notice call an archaeologist;*
   - (c) *How can you tell that there was great interest in the past;*
   - (d) *What does the notice mean by 'marbles'?*

The Victorians were very keen to look at objects from the past. A new British Museum was opened in 1847 to house a growing collection.

Sometimes very elaborate methods had to be used to transport these objects from their places of origin to Britain. The picture on page 14 shows how one object was brought from Egypt to be erected on the Thames Embankment in London.

1. *Where was it found?*
2. *How was it raised?*
3. *How was it transported?*
4. *Do you think it is a good idea to bring objects like this to a place where many people can see them or should they be left where they are found? In your answer you might consider whether a clue can tell you more if it is left exactly in position.*

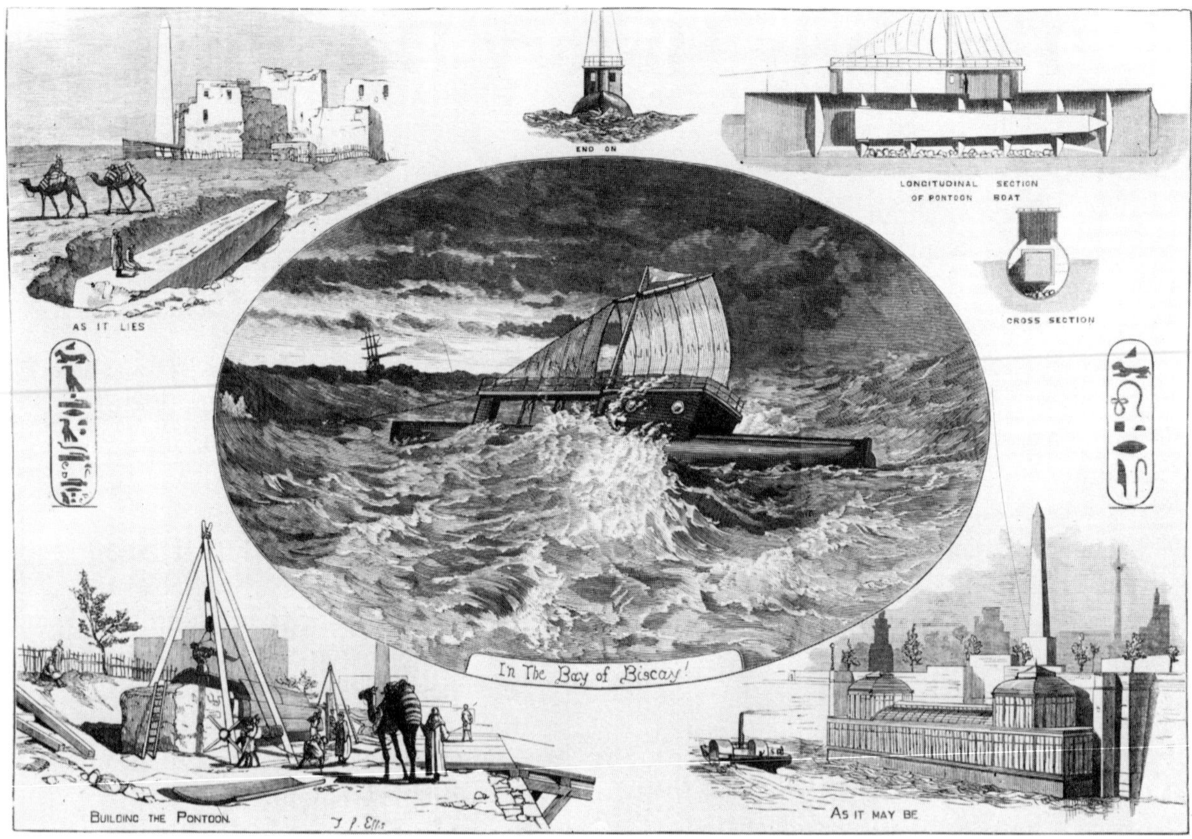

One of the earliest collectors was Giovanni Belzoni, an Italian 203cm [6ft 7ins] tall, who had been a circus strongman before going to Egypt as a hydraulic-pump salesman. He found a job transporting antiquities for the British Museum, and decided to add to the collection by forcing his way with a battering ram into the Pyramid of Khafre.

He said:

the purpose of my researches was to rob the Egyptians of their treasures.

1. *What do you think of Belzoni's qualifications as an archaeologist and of his methods and actions?*

Bible Clues

One reason for early history detective work was simply to acquire objects from the past, out of wealth, possessiveness or curiousity.

Some Victorians also wanted to prove the truth of Bible stories. Henry Layard did just that although it was another book which began his investigations:

My admiration for '*The Arabian Nights*' has never left me. I can read it now with almost as much delight as when I was a boy. It has had a great influence on my life for to it I attribute that love of travel and adventure which took me to the East.

1. *What do you know of 'The Arabian Nights' and its famous adventuring sailor?*

When he was 22, Layard travelled on horseback from England towards Ceylon. He arrived in Turkey and entered a colourful town, beside which stood some huge mounds. These mounds fascinated Layard. He wondered if they might be the broken-down remains of the great city of Nineveh.

1. *What do you know of Nineveh? (See The Bible, Genesis chapter 10, verse 11.)*

Layard gave up his plans to visit Ceylon and instead lived for two years among the people of Turkey finding out about their lives and history. He looked for ancient remains and found many strange stones bearing marks, like this one:

He could not understand them, having had no training as a history detective.

However Layard was determined to make a good job of his investigations. He read about what was happening in Italy at Pompeii and Herculaneum, which had been covered by ash when the volcano Vesuvius erupted in A.D. 79. The Italian history detective, Fiorelli, was taking great care, carefully tunnelling into the hardened ash and using a new method of forcing liquid plaster into various holes. When the plaster dried out came the shape of once living things which had died 1800 years before. The ash had encased these poor victims so perfectly that, as they decomposed, they had left their shapes behind in their ashy shell.

Layard also decided to tunnel into his mounds and came across the palace of King Assurnasipal mentioned in Genesis chapter 10 verse 11. Out of the ruins came beautiful sculptured stones.

Imagine the shock on the faces of the Arab diggers when this huge man-bull appeared out of the ground.

1. *Describe the creature and explain why it terrified the diggers.*
2. *From the onlookers' clothes, where would you say the object has been taken?*

The man-bull object

Layard wrote in his diary:

I was returning to the mound when I saw two Arabs urging their mares to the top of their speed. On approaching me they stopped:
'Master', exclaimed one. 'The diggers have found a monster. On Allah, it is wonderful but it is true. We have seen it with our own eyes!'

An even more dramatic discovery was made. It was a tall pillar called an obelisk covered in pictures and writing telling about the surrender of various princes to King Shalmaneser who had lived in the palace after King Assurnasipal. Here was another direct link with the Bible story of Hoshea, King of Syria.

1. *Look at the picture below. What evidence does it show of Hoshea and his people accepting Shalmaneser as their leader?*

Against him came up Shalmaneser, King of Assyria, and Hoshea became his servant and gave him presents. The King of Assyria took over Syria and Israel. For so it was that the children of Israel had sinned against the Lord their God and had worshipped the statues of the heathen.

II Kings, 17

1. *What do the Bible and Layard's discoveries agree upon?*

Not all of Layard's discoveries were in such good condition as the obelisk. Many objects crumbled away when exposed to the air or to rough handling. Others were lost when the boat carrying them to Britain sunk!

Layard did many things wrong. If he found nothing after digging for a while he left the hole and started elsewhere.

However, he did adopt an orderly system of excavation when he found something. He was not just interested in the value of his finds, but also in what they could tell him about the truth of the Bible.

1. *How would you describe Layard's ideas of history detective work and the quality of his investigations?*

Biblical archaeology still continues to interest many people today. Here are some recent discoveries and investigations.

One of the panels from the Obelisk of Shalmaneser

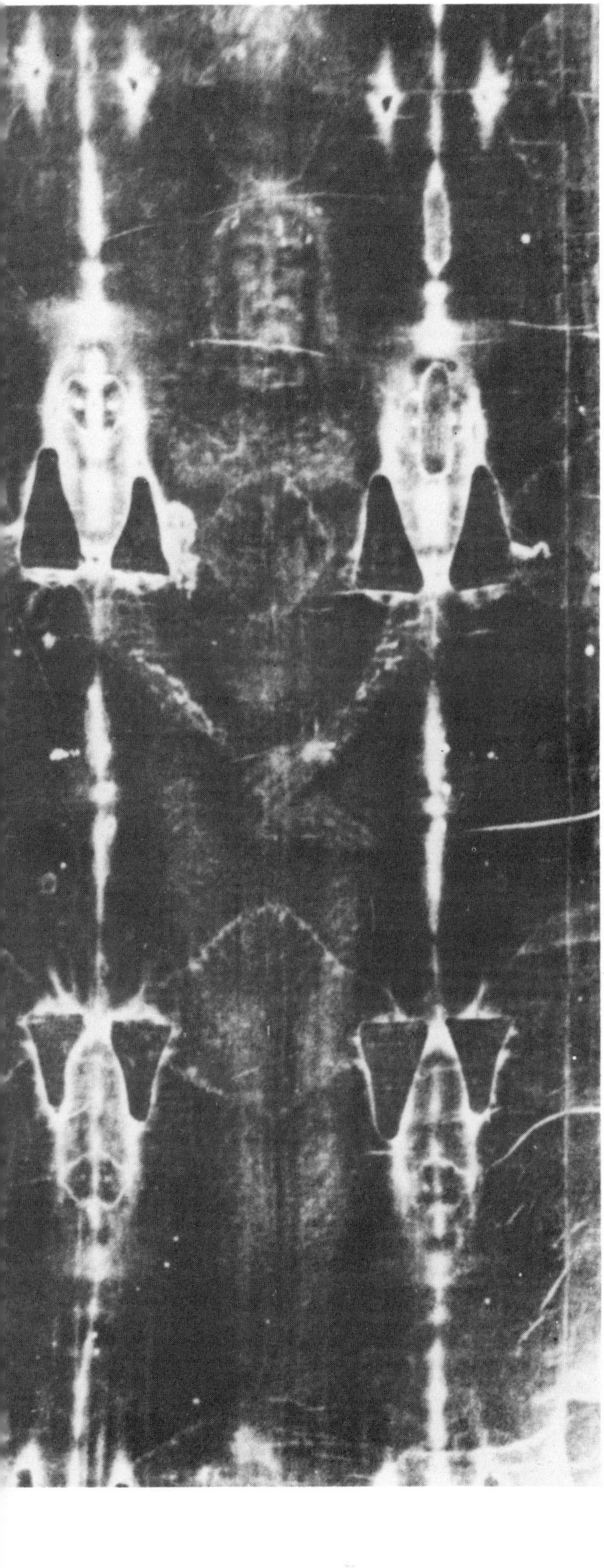

The object on the left is kept in Turin Cathedral, Italy. Is it really the cloth that wrapped Jesus in the tomb after the crucifixion? History detectives have recently investigated this claim, but they are still not absolutely sure.

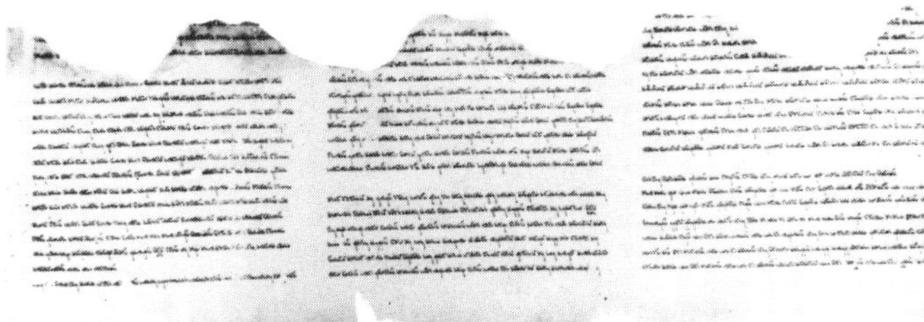

The oldest copy of a manuscript from Biblical times, part of the Scroll of the Children of Light found by chance by an Arab goat-herd in 1947 along the shores of the Dead Sea

A grim raffle ticket? When a group of Jewish resistance-fighters were being attacked by the Romans in AD 73, they decided to die rather than surrender. They drew lots to see who should perform the execution and then kill himself. In 1962, on the site at Masada, near the Dead Sea, were found many skeletons and 11 of these pieces of pottery marked with Jewish names. What might they be?

Truth or Myth

Another reason for undertaking historical detective work was to prove that very old stories had truth in them.

A German investigator Heinrich Schliemann believed that the stories written by the Greek poet, Homer, were based on fact. Many people said that as the stories were 2500 years old and full of Greek myth and legend they were all made up. One of the well known stories was the capture of Helen, daughter of the Greek king Priam, and the subsequent Trojan horse trick to get her back. As a young boy seeing a picture of an attack on the walls of the ancient city of Troy, Schliemann had said to his father:

Papa, if those walls really exist they must still be buried in the dust. One day I'll dig them up.

Schliemann's diary

By the age of 36 Schliemann was a millionaire and able to pursue his lifelong ambition. He had calculated that Troy must lie near Hissarlik in N.W. Turkey and organised investigations of likely sites.

Scholars continued to scorn his ideas but before long the *Illustrated London News* carried this report:

'On the site of Hissarlik [Schliemann has] found Greek masonry and ... pottery, and ... the remains of a wealthy city which had been suddenly destroyed. ... In the ashes of a circuit-wall, close to the mansion of the town's king [were found] skeletons ..., battle-axes, lances daggers and a shield of bronze.'

1. *What evidence was there that Troy had been attacked?*
2. *What evidence was there of Greek influence on the city?*

The most valuable discoveries were found amidst the charred remains of a wooden box. Schliemann dressed his wife, Sophia, in them.

1. *Identify the 'treasures' and describe them.*
2. *What beautiful woman do you think Schliemann claimed they had belonged to?*

Troy did exist! This was a tremendous discovery but Schliemann was not correct when he said he had found Helen's jewels and Priam's palace. He was so intent on proving something that he pushed the evidence too far.

Today we know that Schliemann's Troy was an even older city than the one mentioned by Homer. Schliemann had discovered the earliest of nine cities each built on the ruins of the other. Homer's Troy was later proved to have been the seventh city.

5. The Past-Finders

Early archaeologists were after dramatic discoveries, Biblical proof or treasure and less interested in a careful piecing together of the past. Their investigations were often unscientific and destructive and they tended to make their discoveries fit in with what they wanted to believe. A true discoverer-of-the-past must work slowly and methodically, keeping an open mind and not expecting to discover 'treasure' every time.

A modern history detective is trained in special skills and makes sure of the facts.

A fact is like a sack – it won't stand up until you put something in it.

Carr

1. What does that mean?

Facts must be checked and made to fit all other evidence so that final conclusions are accurate.

To praise [a history detective] for his accuracy is like praising an architect for using well-seasoned timber or properly mixed concrete

Carr

1. What sense do you make of that?

Modern discovery work must be precise. Nothing, however insignificant, can be overlooked because a clue need not be spectacular in order to be valuable. A history detective must work systematically and orderly. All archaeology, for example, is destruction. Once a past layer has been dug into it is destroyed for ever.

1. In our murder in chapter one what would have happened had an untrained person entered the room and tidied it up?

An excavation must be carried out by trained people proceeding carefully through every stage and recording every object in its correct position.

1. What evidence of this care and thoroughness can you see here?

Once an object is found it must be recognised and its similarities or differences to other objects identified. Eight questions need to be asked about an object:

(a) What was it used for?
(b) When was it made?
(c) Where was it made?
(d) How was it constructed?
(e) Where has it been all its life?
(f) Where was it found?
(g) Has it any special meaning?
(i) Has it any artistic value?

1. Which of these eight questions can you answer about the object below, which was found in the Valley of the Tombs of the Kings, Egypt?

The object in the photograph may not look very exciting but, in 1922, it was to lead to a fabulous discovery.

Until 1800 B.C. Egyptian pharaohs [kings] had been buried in huge buildings of stone called pyramids. Despite blocked entrances, secret doors and false passages these tombs had all been robbed.

Later pharaohs ordered that, after death, their bodies should be buried in a remote mountain area far into the desert. One of the architects of this last resting place left an inscription carved into the rock:

I, Ineni, superintended the excavation of these cliff tombs [in the Valley of the Kings] alone, no one seeing or hearing.

1. Why is the history detective pleased to find written evidence?
2. How did Ancient Egyptian writing (hieroglyphics) look?

In 1907 an American archaeologist, Theodore Davis, discovered in the Valley of the Kings an earthenware cup bearing the mark shown here.

1. The sign 'Amen' goes first because it is the name of a God. If you put this symbol after that for 'Ankh', what does the hieroglyphic script say?

Nearby were floral burial collars and a linen shawl bearing the date of Tutankhamen's death, which was 1342 B.C.

1. What evidence was there that Tutankhamen's tomb was in the valley?
2. How long ago did Tutankhamen die?

Very little was known of this pharaoh. If his tomb was found it was doubtful whether there would be anything in it for even in the Valley robbers had entered every one of its 30 burial-chambers.

As the Egyptians believed in an after-life they thought that the dead pharaoh, on his rebirth, would need all his possessions. The temptations presented by these tombs, full of their royal belongings, must have been enormous.

Strange sights the Valley must have seen and desperate ventures: the plotting, the secret meeting on the cliff by night, the bribing or drugging of the cemetery guards, the desperate burrowing in the dark, the scramble through a small hole into the burial-chamber, the hectic search by a glimmering light for treasure that was portable and the return home at dawn laden with booty.

Carter

Howard Carter hoped that one tomb had escaped the thieves — that of Tutankhamen. In 1917 after years of training and excavating in Egypt he received backing from the wealthy Lord Carnarvon. He got permission to carry out history detective work in the Valley of the Kings.

It was a daunting task as the ground was piled high with huge heaps of rubbish from other excavations.

One line of investigation stopped when some twelfth-century B.C. workmen's huts were discovered and where further digging would have blocked the visitors' entrance to the tomb of Pharaoh Rameses VI.

Inquiries began elsewhere but by the winter of 1922 nothing had been found. Carter began to lose heart:

After these barren years were we justified in going on? My own feeling was that so long as a single area of untouched ground remained we should continue. We turned to the workmen's huts area.

1. Why were the old workmen's huts in the Valley?

On 3 November the huts had been cleared. When Carter arrived it was too quiet. Nobody was working. He realised:

that something extraordinary had happened. I was greeted by the announcement that a step cut in the rock had been discovered. The manner of cutting was that of a sunken stairway entrance and I almost dared to hope. . . .

The first step led to another 15, leading downward to

a sealed doorway – it was actually true! Our years of patient labour were going to be rewarded. With excitement growing to fever heat I searched the seal impressions on the door for evidence of their owner but could find no name only the royal necropolis seal [official burial-seal, the object on page 20].

Carter

Two weeks later Lord Carnarvon arrived and the whole door was uncovered. Carter discovered that the lower part of the door did bear Tutankhamen's seal, but that the top half had in fact been broken into and officially resealed, probably about ten years after the original burial. Had the tomb been robbed? Carter was about to find out.

6. Detectives in the Tomb

26 November 1922

The most wonderful day I ever lived through! With trembling hands I made a tiny breach in the corner of the door. Candle tests were applied as a precaution against foul gases and then I inserted the candle and peered in. At first I could see nothing; the hot air escaping from the chamber caused the flame to flicker. Then my eyes grew accustomed to the light and details of the room emerged: strange animals, statues and gold – everywhere the glint of gold. For the moment I was struck dumb with amazement. Lord Carnarvon, unable to stand the suspense inquired anxiously 'Can you see anything?'

It was all I could do to get out the words: 'Yes! Wonderful things!'

Carter

In a chamber measuring 762 X 366 cm was a whole 'museum-full' of objects piled up in total confusion.

1. *See if you can find any of these in the photograph below:*

a lion-headed bed	a quiver of arrows (some with tips missing)
alabaster vases	bows
wooden caskets	boomerangs
egg-shaped boxes of preserved food (duck and venison)	chairs
	stools
a dismantled chariot	torch-holders
jewel cabinets	a stringed instrument

2. *What can you say about Ancient Egyptian life from these finds?*
3. *What evidence is there that robbers had got there first?*

Carter's suspicions of robbery increased when he found a scarf hastily knotted around a handful of gold rings. Furthermore, the objects in some boxes did not match those listed on enclosed documents.

It seems as if the thieves, having been disturbed, ran off leaving the priests to tidy up as best they could and then reseal the tomb with its marvellous collection of objects which Carter was now to investigate.

What thoughts pass through the minds of history detectives when presented with such a discovery?

Carter said:

Time as a factor in human life lost its meaning. 3 000 years had passed since human feet last trod the floor on which I stood and yet, as I noted the signs of recent life around me: the half-filled bowl of mortar for the door, the blackened lamp, the finger-mark upon the freshly painted surface, the farewell-garland dropped upon the threshold, I felt it might have been but yesterday. I felt an intruder. Then came the exhilaration of discovery, the thought that I was about to add a page to history.

1. *Explain the presence of the mortar, lamp, finger-mark and garland?*
2. *Why, according to Carter, is history detective work exciting?*

Carter overcame his natural impulse to rush into the tomb. Instead he went shopping to Cairo for:

Photographic material	labels
chemicals	32 bales of calico
paraffin-wax	2 miles of wadding
packing boxes	1 mile of bandages.

1. *What were they for?*

The Royal Throne

Overlaid with gold from top to bottom the throne was the masterpiece of the first chamber.

The back panel, picked out in silver, red glass, blue porcelain flesh-coloured carnelian and transparent calcite, shows the king in his palace being attended by his wife Ankhesenpaaten who holds a small jar of sweet oil.

1. *How old do the royal couple appear?*
2. *Are they relaxed or formal?*
3. *What symbols of power and kingship are there?*

It took seven weeks to clear the room, every object being first photographed, measured, labelled and then carefully removed. Carter explained:

The objects are not my property. They are a direct legacy from the past to the present age. If by carelessness or ignorance I lessen the sum of knowledge that might be obtained from them I am guilty of a serious crime.

1. *How could Carter have destroyed an object?*
2. *Why would that have been a 'crime'?*

Some objects had to be handled very carefully or they would have crumbled away. They were covered with melted paraffin wax which hardened and allowed the solidified object to be removed. The funeral bouquets were sprayed with a celluloid solution and then removed intact. Some clothes were so rotten that they had to be restored by carefully noting the position of metal buckles, beadwork, sequins, eyelets and rosettes and then reconstructing the garment.

A reconstructed corslet. The beads, jewels and mosaics were found totally scattered. Carter laid them all out on plasticene until he could discover the correct design.

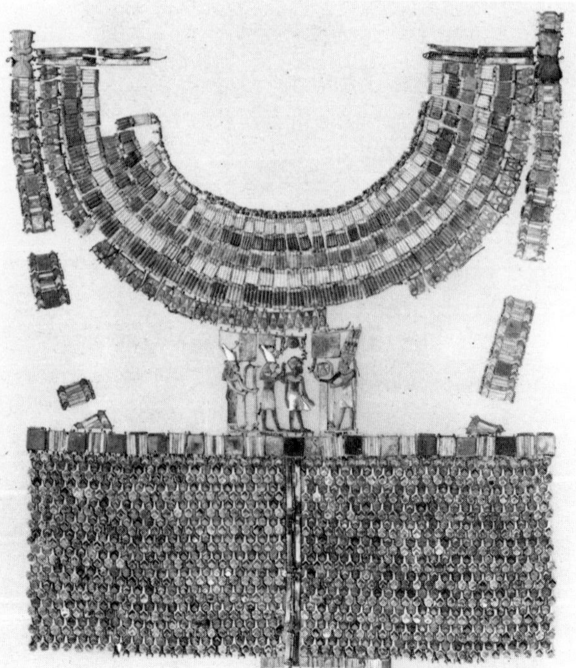

Look at the object in the photograph.

1. *How many separate pieces do you think it has?*
2. *Is it right to restore objects found in poor condition or should they be left as found?*

The work was very time-consuming but Carter knew it was worthwhile.

In all our mending we had constant recourse to our box of floor-sweepings: fragments recovered by sifting the last layer of dust from the floor.

Carter

1. *What boring jobs did Carter do and why?*

The Antechamber cleared, it was time to open a sealed door between guardian statues.

After chipping away the plaster Carter was amazed to come across another barrier; a wall of solid gold! This was the actual burial-chamber of the king surrounded by a huge golden shrine.

Inside was another collection of objects which tell us about the dead pharaoh:
hunting weapons small sandals
loin cloths robes a lock of his childhood hair a wooden walking stick ('cut by his majesty's own hand').

1. *What do these objects tell you about a pharaoh?*
2. *What can you tell about Tutankhamen?*

The pharaoh himself was well protected. Within the shrine was a quartz tomb and inside that a gilded wooden coffin, 213 cm long with Tutankhamen's face in sheet-gold. Underneath was another coffin, 203 cm long covered in a burial-cloth and garlands.

1. *How much shorter was this coffin than the first?*
2. *How do you explain this difference if it fitted perfectly inside the other?*
3. *Why do we put flowers on coffins?*
4. *Who may have placed the simple garland on the head of the coffin?*

Inside was yet a third burial-chest made this time of solid gold, and so heavy it took eight strong men to lift it.

Finding the Body

The lid was raised and there at last was the bandaged body of the king. Over the 'mummy' had been poured anointing oil which had solidified and blackened with age. In contrast was a brilliant golden mask:

> a beautiful and unique specimen . . . bearing a sad but calm expression of youth overtaken prematurely with death.
>
> Carter

1. *What two creatures on the mask represent the kingdoms of Egypt?*
2. *Why had sticky oil been poured over the mummy?*

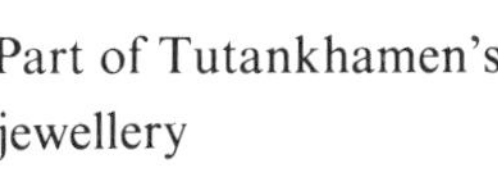

Part of Tutankhamen's jewellery

Tutankhamen's mask

3. *Describe the king from his mask.*

Carefully the bandages and linen pads were unwrapped. Mixed in with them were 143 objects of beautifully made jewellery. Many bore designs of serpents, vultures, scarab beetles, hawks and herons. Some depicted a strange, painted eye and other weird symbols.

1. *What do they tell you about the skill of Egyptian craftsmen?*
2. *Were they just for decoration?*

One clue as to the meaning of the jewellery comes from the 'Book of the Dead' which often appears painted in tombs:

A man remains over after death. Existence yonder is for eternity and . . . for him who reaches it . . . he shall exist like a God . . . .

Whoever wears the Emblem of Osiris may enter into the realms of the dead and eat the food of Osiris, the ruler of the Otherworld. . . .

The Book of the Dead

1. *What did the Ancient Egyptians believe happened after death?*
2. *Who was Tutankhamen's jewellery to impress?*

Some jewellery was probably also placed in the tomb to protect the wearer on the journey to the 'Otherworld'.

Life after death was only possible, however, if the body did not disappear into dust, but was properly preserved.

The early stages of 'mummification' involved the removal of the internal organs and their preservation in special urns called canopic jars. The body was then filled with sweet-smelling herbs and steeped in natron [preserving salt] for 70 days.

The bandaged mummy was then put into its painted coffin while priests chanted magic spells and placed special objects on it. These ceremonies were to help the dead pharaoh on his 'journey'.

If the soul reached the otherworld it still had to undergo another test before it could join its body.

The Weighing of the Soul

1. *Look at the picture below and find:*
   (a) *The God Anubis, in charge of the weighing;*
   (b) *The scales weighing the 'soul' in its 'canopic' jar.*
   (c) *Thoth, the scribe, recording the result;*
   (d) *The 'Devourer of Souls' waiting to eat the soul if it fails the test, being 'too heavy' with evil.*
   (e) *Horus, the falcon-headed God with the magic-eye, pictured on some jewellery.*
2. *How is the soul's fate literally 'in the balance'?*

The weighing of the soul from *The Book of the Dead*

Did Tutankhamen pass the tests and enter the Otherworld? His body was not actually very well preserved as the anointing-oils had caused the flesh to burn. This was discovered when the investigators removed the last piece of bandaging and exposed the body.

Medical Report on the Unwrapped Mummy of Tutankhamen

Head	clean-shaven; white salt-spots
Skull cavity	empty
Nostrils	plugged with material
Lips	slightly raised
Teeth	large central; wisdom teeth just through
Ears	small, pierced
Body	165cm long; 86mm opening in abdomen
Bones	not fully grown (aged about 18)

1. What do you deduce from this report?

The original examination found no reason for Tutankhamen's death. Recently however an X-ray revealed a large depression in the skull. Was Tutankhamen murdered? He certainly lived during an unruly period of Egyptian history, but there we run out of clues and must close the files on the pharaoh, Tutankhamen.

(left) The head of Tutankhamen's mummy as first revealed.
(right) Tutankhamen's mummy as it first appeared to Howard Carter

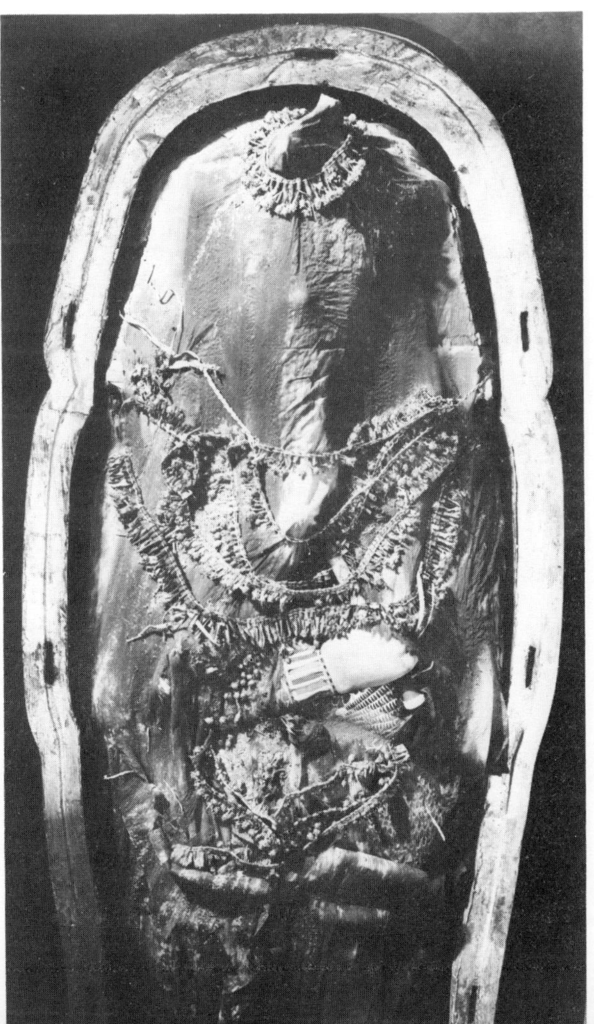

7. Science to the Rescue

The Tutankhamen discovery was unique and dramatic: a time-capsule preserved in the dry air of a tomb. It was easy to date the objects because they were all buried at the same time. Elsewhere this is not so easy and so it is even more important to record exactly where an object is found.

Stratigraphy means studying the way in which layers of earth have been laid down over many years. In this way the history detective finds clues showing what happened on a site at different periods in the past.

1. *Look at the picture. Put these finds in order from oldest to most recent.*

2. *Why is a rubbish pit (B) a useful discovery?*
3. *Explain the existence of the layer of ash (C).*
4. *Why are the crops above ground of different heights? How can this help the history detective?*

Usually the older the object, the deeper down in an excavation it is found.

1. *Explain why you must be careful about dating a burial (A).*

The history detective is limited by what he finds. No objects were made to be historic documents or preserved especially to help the finder.

The modern investigator has many new scientific methods to help him, such as magnetic-dating of pottery, infra-red photography, metal analysis, tree-ring dating, aerial photography, resistivity surveying.

Carter had none of these aids available to him. Many of his methods are now questioned, but we must give him credit for what he did during years of careful research, painstaking work and imaginative, detailed writing.

8. The Mystery of the Mary Rose

We have found that through careful history detective work we can understand the past and develop skills which can benefit us in many ways, helping us to:

(a) understand how and why things have happened;
(b) widen our experience from reliving the lives of other people;
(c) appreciate the world in which we live;
(d) ask questions about why people do things and whether we would do the same.

There were three problems concerning the *Mary Rose* which had sunk, watched by King Henry VIII, in 1545 off Southsea Castle, near Portsmouth.

Problem 1 Where exactly was the sunken wreck?
Problem 2 Why had it sunk?
Problem 3 What could it reveal about life on a Tudor warship?

Problem 1 Where was the wreck?

The whereabouts of the ship had been known in the past but, by 1976, all trace of it had disappeared. History detective Alexander McKee determind to find it again. His researches led him to the Admiralty Hydrographic Department in London where he found an old naval chart.

It took ten seconds to unroll and then I leaned forward . . . and there it was: a red cross and the name, *Mary Rose*, in 6 fathoms.* I gave an audible gasp.

1. What exactly did Mckee find?
2. How far down was the ship?

A sonar scan of the likely area revealed something beneath the thick mud and divers went down hoping to find evidence that it was indeed the *Mary Rose*.

**1 fathom = 6 feet (1.83 m)*

Eventually one diver brought up a sausage-shaped object encrusted with debris, which after careful cleaning looked like this:

It was a cannon from the *Mary Rose*. The ship had been found preserved in the silt of the Solent. It appeared that the ship had been prepared for battle, but had sunk unexpectedly and quickly. The old engraving on page 29 confirms that fact.

1. *Look at the scene and identify:*
   (a) The leading English ship The Great Harry;
   (b) Four French oared-galleys attacking the English;
   (c) Henry VIII about to enter Southsea Castle;
   (d) The sunken Mary Rose.
2. *What signs of disaster can you see?*

Problem 2 Why had the ship sunk so suddenly?

Make useful notes from these statements from four witnesses:

(A) Marshal du Bellay, with the French fleet:

> Fortune favoured us . . . for the *Mary Rose*, one of their principal ships, was sunk by our cannon and of the 600 men on board only five and thirty escaped.

(B) Sir George Carew, Vice-Admiral on the *Mary Rose* (speaking before he went down with his ship):

> I have the sort of knaves I cannot rule. It is a case of 'the more cooks, the worse pottage'. See how the sails are mismanaged.

(C) Sir Peter Carew (Sir George's nephew) commenting on the ship's normal crew of 120 mariners, 250 soldiers, 20 gunners, 5 trumpeters and 35 servants):

> There were 700 on board that day, and many in full armour. This made the ship to heel.

(D) A Portsmouth boatwright who had helped at the ship's refit in 1536:

> I remember the problem we had cutting gun-ports in the new hull. It was hard to make them watertight. It seemed odd to be cutting holes low in the side of a ship. I remember saying that I hoped the ship would not lean over with its gun-holes left open.

A one-sided view is called **bias** and the history detective must be able to spot it so that the truth can be detected.

1. *Is anyone expressing an opinion not really based on evidence? Explain your answer.*
2. *Using all the evidence you have now work out a probable cause of the disaster.*

Problem 3 What can we learn from the wreck about shipboard life?

I was swimming along . . . when I looked down into a hole [and] . . . came face to face with a skull. It gave me quite a fright. Margaret Rule [chief archaeologist] wrote down that it was the skull of an archer. They had found next to it some perfectly preserved longbows and a quiver of arrows.

Prince Charles

1. *What evidence is there of:*
   (a) The speed of the sinking;
   (b) An archer's equipment?
2. *Why did Margaret Rule have to write down her information?*
3. *How does the underwater history detective overcome other problems such as breathing, making grids, removing debris and bringing up objects?*

One find on the ship helped to solve another mystery. In other excavations on land circles of leather like the one below had been found. Nobody was sure what they were.

1. *How did these finds solve the problem?*

Methods of preservation have improved dramatically since Howard Carter's day. Computers now decide the best method to use: freeze drying, steeping in polyethylene glycol, polyester resins or a metal stabilising hydrogen furnace.

On the Mary Rose some objects had vanished but had left behind 'negative casts' from which moulds were made using silicone rubber.

(above) A bundle of tightly-bound arrows from the *Mary Rose*. It is very important to preserve these objects as soon as they are brought up from the sea-bottom.
(top) An underwater history detective examines a find from the *Mary Rose*.

1. *What earlier technique does this remind you of?* *(See page 15.)*

Some of the 17000 objects found in this sixteenth-century time-capsule will help us to find out what a sailor's life was like.

bones from: fish, sheep, chickens, pigs, rats, a dog and a fighting-cock

rough wooden bowls   drinking mugs   silver table-ware   pewter flagons and cutlery   huge copper pot   leather buckets   glassware
fire bricks   Scottish silver birch logs   spice grinder   candlesticks

leather gloves   arm protectors and jerkins (showing chain mail stitch points)
leather shoes (sheep skin uppers)
woollen beret and stockings   barber-surgeon's cap

amputation-saw handles   bleeding bowl   heavy mallet   medicine bottles
razors   syringes   mortar and pestle   brass scales   pocket sundial   compass dividers

fishing tackle   brass thimbles   sharpening-stone

powder-shovel   linstock (for holding a slow-burning taper)

gun-rammers   (to push in shot etc)   24 of the original 91 guns (all loaded)

gaming board   dice   ivory book-spine   bone carvings

1. *Which items belonged to: archers, gunners, officers, common sailors, sailmaker, ship's doctor.*
2. *What can you deduce from:*
   (a) the bones;
   (b) the logs?
3. *What can you say about Tudor naval food, clothing, weapons, hygiene, medicine, pleasures?*
4. *Compare an officer's life to a common sailor's.*

What you have been doing is reconstructing life on board a Tudor warship. This is the high point of the historian's craft. It involves all the skills which we have been looking at and it requires quite detailed factual knowledge of the past.

9. Researching Family Facts

A history detective patiently searches for any clue which will help to construct a picture of the past, even the information gained from a family history investigation.

I wondered what I could discover about my mother's family, the Cockburns. My first clue came from my grandfather, James Cockburn, born in 1876, the fifth in a family of nine children. He told me, and it was confirmed in our old Family Bible, that he came from a croft near Fyvie in Aberdeenshire and that his father, George, had died in 1884.

Write the missing words in your own book.

1. *George Cockburn was my ________*
2. *When his father died James was ________ old.*
3. *His mother (called Mary Tough) found life hard because ________ .*

The next step was to search Fyvie graveyard. On a headstone I found my great-great-grandfather, Alexander. From the headstone I could work out that:

1. *He had been born in ________.*
2. *His son, (my great-grandfather) George, had been born in ________ .*

Erected in memory of
Alexander Cockburn
Died 24th May 1867
aged 73 years
and of his wife
Isabel Cruikshank
who died 24th Jan 1862
aged 64 years
Also of their son George
who died 27th June 1884
aged 48 years
and his wife, Mary Tough
died 3rd Dec 1925, aged 79

It was likely that Alexander had been born in the same parish and that his birth would be recorded in the church register. I knew which date to look for and I knew where to find the evidence — in the Record Office in Edinburgh. There I found that the Old Parish Register of Fyvie had been copied on to microfilm which I had to read through a special magnifying viewer.

Eventually I found the entry I wanted:

> *1794 June 6th Alexander, son to William Cockburn and Jane Marr*

The church session-clerk had recorded the name of Alexander's father, 'William', my great-great-great grandfather. This clue led me back to Fyvie churchyard and this stone:

1. *What evidence is there that this* William *is my ancestor?*
2. *In which year was he born?*

I could now return to the Old Parish Register and search in the mid-eighteenth century. I found — nothing!

There were no Cockburns at all before the year 1790. Where had they come from? Where had William been born?

I tried other Aberdeenshire parishes but without success. The name Cockburn is not an Aberdeenshire name. In the 1696 Poll Book recording all taxpayers in that county not a single Cockburn appears.

Then I remembered an old family story claiming that the name Cockburn comes from the name, Gowk's Burn, a stream in Berwickshire.

I looked up a map of this area.

1. *What useful clues can you find on the map?*
2. *What is the largest town on the map?*

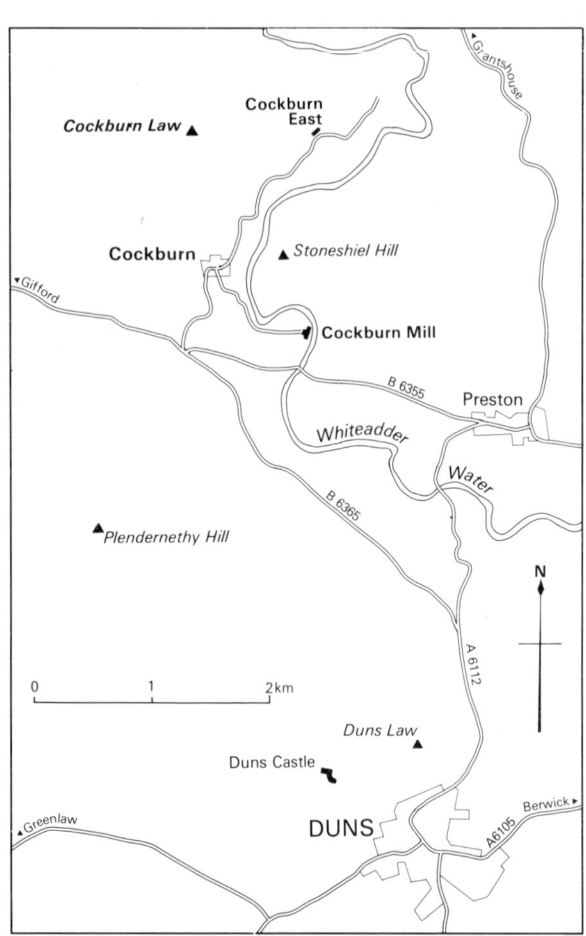

In the Duns Church register I found this extract:

> *1756 1st February William Cockburn born to Alexander Cockburn and Christian Kay.*

I cannot be absolutely certain that this William is my great-great-great grandfather, but the name and date are right and the area fits in with family tradition.

Oral history — the passing down of information from one generation to the next — must never be underestimated. It was the *only* clue that black American Alex Haley had to go on. His slave-ancestors did not know exactly where they came from or where their roots were. However, there was a tradition about the founder of the family, an African.

> His name was Kintay. 'He say . . . de river [where he came from] de 'Kamby Bolongo' an' he was choppin' wood to make hissel' a drum when dey cotched him.'
>
> Haley

1. *Who caught Kintay?*

How Alex Haley did his family detective work and discovered his ancestors in Gambia makes fascinating reading in his book, *Roots.*

If my family story is true and the Duns connection is correct then William's father was Alexander (born 1726) and his mother was Christian Kay. Before that the clues run out. The older registers are difficult to

Alexander (b.1726) = Christian Kay
William (1756-1847) = Jane Marr
Alexander (1794-1867) = Isabel Cruikshank
George (1836-1884) = Mary Tough
James (1876-1957)

(= means 'married')

(| means 'child of')

read and frequently key-entries are missing, destroyed by fire or flood, eaten by mice or just lost.

I have been able to fill in many more names, but a simple form of family tree is shown above.

One of the exciting things about tracing a family tree is being able to fill in some 'historical foliage' around the bare branches.

William must have left Duns about 1788. What made a 32-year-old man uproot himself from the Borders of Scotland and journey hundreds of miles on foot over primitive roads to an uncertain future in the bleak moors of the North?

One answer comes from a comparison of the two areas. One way of doing this is by consulting the *Statistical Accounts* written by the ministers of Duns and Fyvie in the 1790s.

DUNS PARISH

40 sq. miles [104 sq km]:
all cultivated.
Pop. *1750* *1790*
2593 3324
Scholars: 100
Poor roll: 90
Farms worth £30–£100: 14
Farms worth £100–£300: 14
Crops grown: wheat, barley, oats, potatoes, cabbage
3 large fairs a year (£28,000 of cattle sold)

FYVIE PARISH

104 sq. miles (269 sq km):
30 (78) cultivated
Pop. *1750* *1790*
2538 2194
Scholars: 40
Poor roll: 24
Farms worth £30–£100: 12
Farms worth £100–£300: 1
Crops grown: oats, wild barley
A few small rural markets

1. *Summarise the conditions of the two areas saying which is the richer.*

In Duns the period of farming improvement called the **Agricultural Revolution** was complete. The farming **Improvers** had abolished the old-fashioned, open-strip farming and changed to large fields enclosed by hedges and dykes [walls]. Everything was more efficient and machinery was increasingly replacing people, leaving less room for the small farmers, who found it hard to survive.

1. *How does the Duns report confirm this fact?*

Faced with this situation, perhaps, William decided to seek his fortune elsewhere. It is possible that the Cockburn family had some connection with the Gordons who were powerful in Aberdeenshire. Certainly William Gordon, Lord Haddo, was keen to invite newcomers, especially from progressive areas like Berwickshire, to help him improve his farming.

Liberal encouragement has been given to the tenants by draining, liming, enclosing, building houses and making roads.

Lord Haddo in his *Estate Records*

1. *What improvements was Lord Haddo making?*

At first William must have worked as a 'fee'd man' for others. He is not recorded renting land himself until 1828.

WILLIAM COCKBURN,
WOODHEAD FARM

	£	s	d
1828: Money rental:	2	0	0
2 hens worth		2	0
towards school			1
Lease expires: 1844			

1. *For how long was William's lease of Woodhead?*
2. *Previously leases had lasted one year. Why was a longer lease an advantage to the farmer?*

By 1840 the *Fyvie New Statistical Account* was able to say:

The population is 3927. The chief cause is the reclaiming of waste land and the formation of new settlements,

1. *What is the evidence that Fyvie is flourishing?*

At Woodhead William also prospered but the croft could not support all his five sons. When he died one son took over the croft as we can see in the document below.

1. *What is a census?*
2. *Describe the family now living at Woodhead.*
3. *William died in 1847 having lived under five monarchs. Who were they?*

Meanwhile where was William's second son, Alexander, my great-great-grandfather? The map on page 37 which shows a remote corner of the Haddo estates will help.

1. *What is the area called?*
2. *What does that name, and others, tell you about conditions in the area?*
3. *How many acres were ploughed?*

1851 Census Woodhead

NAME	POSITION	STATUS	AGE	OCCUPATION
George Cockburn	Head	married	51	Farmer of 20 acres
Ann Cockburn	Wife	married	48	Housewife
George Cockburn	Son	unmarried	25	Farm servant
Mary Cockburn	Daughter	unmarried	18	Farm servant
Margaret Cockburn	Daughter	unmarried	5	Scholar

Ten years later the number of cultivated acres had risen to five, showing the pitiful slowness with which the croft was reclaimed from the moss.

What was life like on the croft?

The picture which emerges from sources like school log-books, diaries, local histories and surveys of agriculture is one of great poverty: of evenings around a peat-fire with its hanging kail pot [cauldron or stock pot]: the guid-man [husband] dressed in rough sark [vest], wincey shirt and homespun tweeds, sitting smoking his pipe in the one good chair; his wife in woollen skirt, sacking apron, blouse and shawl taking oatmeal from the girnel [meal chest] to soak overnight; the bairns on chaff-filled mattresses in the loft.

In the morning after porridge, a wash in the porch-pail and a visit to the outside privy, the children would set off, in well-mended breeks [breeches or trousers] or patched pinafores, to the one-roomed school with its bench-desks. Their father would trudge towards his sour parcel of land with its crop of neeps [turnips] or oats and, with primitive tools, battle against the soil and weather in a constant struggle to make ends meet.

1. *What do the words underlined mean?*
2. *Imagine that you are living on this croft at harvest time. Write about your life.**

*Extra information can be found in *The Edwardians*, *Young Workers in the Industrial Revolution* and *Country People in the Agricultural Revolution* from *Exploring History* series.

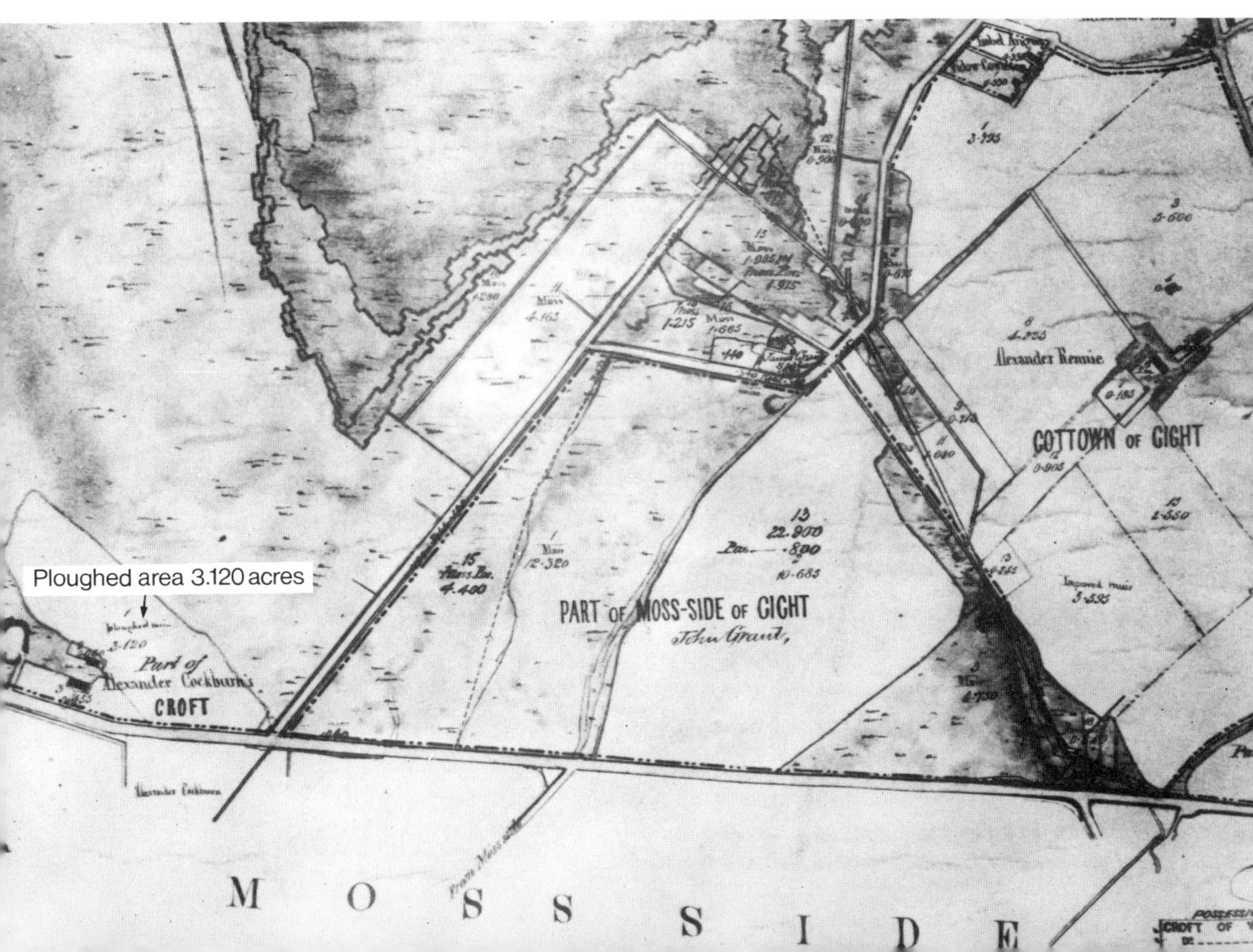

Life on the croft worsened during a period of bad harvests in the late nineteenth and early twentieth centuries. Alexander died in 1867 and his son, George, in 1884. George's wife, Mary Tough, and her son (also George), tried to keep Mosshead going. Another son, James (my grandfather), joined a Royal Artillery Transport Company and fought in the First World War.*

His younger brother Robert (born 1878) joined the Navy. As he remembered much later:

One drizzly afternoon in 1893 I stood on Aberdeen-Quay gazing across at the black hulk of the *Clyde*, the naval reserve drill ship. I saw a boat putting off. 'Mister, how can I gang on board your ship?'

'Oh you're that Fyvie lad that wrote me about joining the navy. Get in my boat.'

I was taken to the mess and given a much better dinner than I had been used to. Some lads showed me how to sling my hammock. I got into it and cuddled down for the night.

1. *How old was Robert on joining the Navy?*
2. *How would you have felt in his position?*
3. *Why was his first naval meal better than usual?*
4. *Try interviewing an old person with an interesting story.*

Robert fought against the German Kaiser's High Seas Fleet in the 1914-18 war and rose from cabin boy to Lieutenant-Commander. After the war he stayed in the Navy while James took a job as mechanic-chauffeur for Sir William Baird of Leuchie, North Berwick—back near 'Cockburn country'.

There he married Annie McIsaac, the daughter of Sir William's gamekeeper. One of their three children was my mother, Mary.

1. *Copy out my family tree and add any extra names found in this chapter.*
2. *Draw your own family tree going back as far as you can.*

**See top left photograph on front cover (standing centre)*

10. Be a Local Detective

We have been looking at clues from two types of sources:

Primary Sources original material dating from the past time being studied

Secondary Sources not actually dating from the past event they describe.

1. *Are these Primary or Secondary Sources?*
   (a) *Fyvie Parish Register of Births, Marriages and Deaths (1726–1790)*
   (b) *The Statistical Account of Duns*
   (c) *The New Forest: its History and Scenery by Herbert R Wise, published 1862*
   (d) *The Census of 1851*
   (e) *Alexander Cockburn's Headstone in Fyvie Graveyard*
   (f) *A photograph of your great grand-mother around the time of World War One*
   (g) *The mock-up of the interior of a But and Ben from the Agricultural Museum at Ingliston*
2. *Try to find a copy of an old newspaper, school log-book, town council minute, local history book or, if you live in Scotland, a copy of your town's* Statistical Accounts *(Old and New).*
3. *What other sources are there to help you discover your own area?*
4. *Visit your local graveyard.*

Mock-up of the interior of a but and ben (Agricultural Museum, Ingliston)

Gravestones

This last suggestion may seem peculiar but remember how we have already found graveyards useful. There are many more clues to look for there:

Christian names, common in the past, no longer used;
old trades once flourishing in your area;
old surnames revealing old trades.

1. *What trade was performed by men with these surnames:* Webster, Smith, Mason, Cooper, Wright, Miller, Baxter, Fletcher, Lorimer?
2. *What other names which are jobs can you think of?*

Some stones are decorated with the tools of the trade.

1. *What do you think the tools in photographs A, B and C represent?*
2. *How do these old carvings help the historian?*

A

B

C

Other carvings tell us about our ancestors' ideas and beliefs and represent the passing of time or the passing of a soul to heaven:

1. *In photographs D, E and F look for symbols of:*
   - (a) *Old Father Time with his scythe;*
   - (b) *hourglasses, measuring the passing of time;*
   - (c) *winged souls;*
   - (d) *an angel with a sword of death;*
   - (e) *death-head skull and other bones;*

D

E

F

Your local cemetery might have some military headstones in it.

Look at this one:

1. *What was the soldier's name and rank?*
2. *What was his regiment and regimental motto?*
3. *What was the date of death and the soldier's age?*

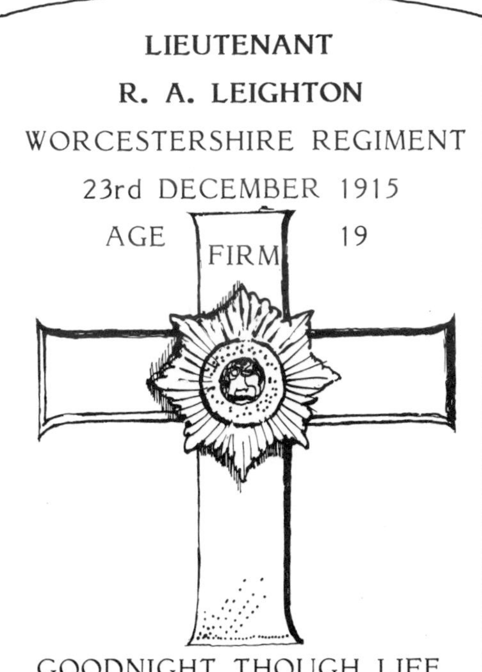

4. *What is the religious symbol?*
5. *What is the inscription chosen by relatives?*
6. *In which war was he killed?*

In fact this headstone is not in a British cemetery but at Louvencourt in France. Although some First World War graves do exist in Britain most soldiers were buried where they fell.

The Commonwealth War Graves Commission looks after British war-graves throughout the world. Whether it marks the burial place of a general or a private, a military headstone is always the same: of Portland stone 2'8" high × 1'3" wide [81cm × 38cm].

Every stone has a story to tell. Roland Leighton was engaged to marry Vera Brittain. On Christmas Eve, 1915, she was expecting him home on leave. She wrote about what happened in her book *Testament of Youth:*

A message came to say I was wanted on the telephone. Believing that I was at last to hear the voice for which I had waited for twenty-four hours I dashed joyously into the corridor. But the message was not from Roland, but from his mother . . . to tell me he had died of wounds at a casualty clearing station at Louvencourt on December 23rd.

Brittain

You could try one of these projects:

- *(a) Research a 'story' from your local cemetery;*
- *(b) Read how Roland Leighton died in* Testament of Youth;
- *(c) Visit battlefields and war-graves on the continent;*
- *(d) Talk to or tape a local survivor from the Great War.*

Views of the past

Talking to an old person about the past is always a useful exercise. Perhaps they might be able to show you some old pictures, which you can compare to the same view today.

1. What differences can you see between these two pictures of Linlithgow?

Try to find some old pictures of your area to compare with today's view.

Another good source of old views is picture postcards. Early cards, from 1894, had the message written around the picture on the front. In 1902 the Post Office allowed the postcard to be divided on the back, half for name and address and half for a message.

Between then and 1914 about 7 800 000 000 postcards were sent in Britain. You should still be able to find plenty of them!

1. *Imagine that you are living in 1910 when the top postcard was sent. What is life like in this Dorsetshire village, do you think?*
2. *Now imagine that you have gone to London on holiday. You send the postcard below to a friend in the country. Write a message describing how you find life in the big city.*

Reconstructions

Recreating the past in this way requires the careful collection of clues and the accurate reconstruction of past events and life styles. It is easy to make mistakes.

1. *Can you spot any mistakes in the above reconstruction of a British kitchen in 1914? If so, what are they?* (Answers on page 47.)

Putting something in the wrong period of time is called an **anachronism**. Every recreated event must carefully avoid showing anything which is not in harmony with the period being recreated.

1. *What sort of detail would you need to know if you were staging a Victorian canal-trip like the one below?* (You could find some of the answers on the following pages or from other books in the *Exploring History* series.)

Working life in the past

An awareness of the past will always keep you interested in your environment. History is all around you: in local place-names, in traditional customs, in old buildings: castles, factories, mills, canals and industrial relics. The study of the remains of past working-life is called **Industrial Archaeology**.

1. *What interesting reminders of old industries could you study in your area?*
2. *What help could you get in this study from: maps, photographs, diaries, trade - directories, newspapers, interviews, business records and accounts, parliamentary papers, local histories?*

Think how an extract like the following — from an official report of the Children's Employment Commission 1843 — would help the history detective.

Sedgeley, near Wolverhampton.

The nature of the occupation of the children . . . is almost entirely that of nail-making at the forge. Many of the workshops are at the back of the hovels in which the working class live. . . . They present the appearance of a dilapidated coal-hole or little black den, in which work seven or eight individuals with no ventilation except the door and two slits or loop-holes in the wall.

These little work places have the forge placed in the centre, round which they have barely standing room at an anvil. Men and women and boys and girls [have] to clamber over each other's bodies or else step upon hot cinders to get over the forge in order to reach the door.

The effluvia [*smells*] of these dens, from the filthiness of the ground, from the half-ragged, half-naked unwashed persons at work and from the hot smoke ashes, water and clouds of dust are really dreadful.

(You can find out more evidence about past working conditions in *Young Workers in the Industrial Revolution.*)

1. *Can you believe the evidence from this official report?*
2. *What would the person writing the report want to happen because of his comments?*
3. *What kind of evidence might you have got from the owner of the forge?*

All evidence must be examined very carefully. The history detective must always ask searching questions about the accuracy of any information. It is important to discover whether evidence is not telling the whole story and is therefore biased in some way.

The more you study evidence the easier it becomes to spot inaccuracies. The amount of information available is immense. It has only been possible in this book to look at some of the sources which history detectives can use. As discovery techniques get more and more scientific new ways of studying the past will be invented. Already objects are being examined using high-power X-rays, laser beams and electron-scanners. Computers also are increasingly being used.

1. *Try to remember how the following sources of evidence were used in the book:*
   - *(a) early written sources;*
   - *(b) discovered objects;*
   - *(c) newspapers, books including the Bible;*
   - *(d) burials;*

(e) *maps, charts, estate plans and papers;*
(f) *registers, statistical accounts, censuses;*
(g) *engravings pictures and photographs;*
(h) *official reports, diaries and log books;*
(i) *eye-witnesses and reminiscences;*
(j) *marks left by man;*

2. *How would these sources be useful to the history detective?*
   (a) *minute books, inventories and wills (lists of possessions);*
   (b) *account books and household books;*
   (c) *family papers;*
   (d) *royal charters;*
   (e) *travellers' descriptions;*
   (f) *church papers and monks' chronicles?*
3. *What other evidence would help you to study the past?*

Every day new material becomes available. The work of the history detective in making sense of it and learning from it is never ending. I hope that you will always continue to be a history detective.

The History Detective Crossword

Copy out this grid into your book and then answer the clues, most of which can be found in the pages of this book.

Across

1. A collection of objects from the same period (4 and 7)
6. Leakey's word for early ape-men (8)
7. Not used for propelling sailing ships (6)
10. (2nd part of 21 across) (4)
11. Crofters lived in a but and . . . (3)
12. Digging in the Valley of the Kings was ______ hot (4)
16. Grauballe Man died by having ____ ________ ____ (3, 6, 3)
17. Arranging dates in the correct order (10)
20. An Italian volcano, not Vesuvius (4)
21. *and* 10 *across* A ship sunk (4 and 4)
22. What preserved the above ship? (4)
24. Archaeologists often dig beneath one (5)
25. They stole from graves (7)
27. In the Year of Our Lord (abbreviation, 2)

Down

1. Burial places (5)
2. Where coins are made (4)
3. It had to be broken to read Shalmaneser's obelisk (4)
4. What held the internal organs of dead pharaohs? (4)
5. What a history detective uses to prove his case (8)
6. Buried in ash along with Pompeii (11)
8. Tutankhamen's nationality (8)
9. Time taken for the earth to go round the sun (4)
13. A daily journal (5)
14. Period when man used flint tools (5 and 3)
15. Horse-drawn canal boats (6)
17. An official count of the population (6)
18. Early history detective (6)
19. What history detectives search for (5)
23. Opposite of even (3)
26. Before Christ (abbreviation, 2)

Bibliography and Abbreviation of Sources

Primary Sources

1696 Aberdeenshire Poll Book, Spalding Club, Aberdeen University Press.

Census of Scotland, 1851

Gight Estate records, Haddo House and Register House, Edinburgh.

New Statistical Account of 1844

Parish Registers (Public Record Office, Edinburgh)

The Illustrated London News (I.L.N.)

The Holy Bible, King James version.

The Statistical Account of Scotland, Vols 4 and 9.

Secondary Sources

E. Bacon (ed) *The Great Archeologists*, Bobbs-Merrill Co. Ltd, 1976

E. Bradford *The Story of the Mary Rose*, Hamish Hamilton (in association with the *Mary Rose* Trust), 1982

H. Bradley *A Handbook of Coins of the British Isles*, Robert Hale, 1978

V. Brittain *Testament of Youth*, Collins Fontana, 1979

J.M. Bulloch *House of Gordon*, Vol. I, New Spalding Club, Aberdeen University Press, 1903

A. D. Cameron *History for Young Scots*, Books I and 2, Oliver & Boyd, 1980

E.H. Carr *What is History?*, Pelican, 1964

H. Carter *The Tombs of Tutankhamen*, Sphere Books, 1972

L. Casson *Ancient Egypt*, Time-Life International, 1966

W. Duval and V. Monaghan *Collecting Postcards*, Blandford Press, 1978

T.R. Entwhistle *Picture Facts: Ancient World*, Galley Press, 1981

D. Forbes *Life before Man*, A & C Black, 1959

R.A. Gale *Prehistoric Life*, Macdonald Educational, 1973

P.V. Glob *The Bog People*, (trans. R. Bruce-Mitford), Faber & Faber, 1977

C. Goff *Archaeology*, Macdonald, 1973

A. Haley *Roots*, Hutchinson, 1977

J. Justice (ed) *Archaeology*, (*New Horizon Library*), Sampson Low, 1976

Larousse Encylopaedia of Archaeology, Hamlyn, 1972

P. Leakey *The Making of Mankind*, Michael Joseph, 1981

J. Pratt *Buchan*, Lewis Smith, 1870

R.A. Rahtz *Rescue Archaeology*, Penguin, 1974

Schools Council *History Around Us*, Holmes McDougall, 1976

A. Smith (ed) *A New History of Aberdeenshire*, Lewis Smith, 1875

P. Vernus *Times of the Pharaohs*, Hart-Davis, 1980

B. Willsher & D. Hunter *Stones: Eighteen-Century Scottish Gravestones*, Canongate, 1978

Additionally, reference is made to books in the *Exploring History* series

Answers

The Anachronism Question (page 44)

The Zip on the lady's skirt and the yo-yo in the girl's hand. This is because these were not invented until 1919 and 1929.

The other items on the page were invented as follows:
The milk bottle, 1906; Kelloggs Cornflakes, 1898; Hoover cleaner, 1907; electric cooker, 1893; electric kettle, 1891; Swan electric light, 1880; electric iron, 1892; mincer, 1896; Vim cleanser, 1905; Cadbury's Dairy Milk, 1902; Players Cigarettes, 1892; Oxo cubes, 1899; teddy bear, 1902; Meccano 1901.

Crossword Solution

Across
1. time capsule; 6. hominids; 7. engine; 10. Rose; 11. ben; 12. very; 16. his throat cut; 17. chronology; 20. Etna; 21. Mary; 22. silt; 24. mound; 25. robbers; 27. A.D.

Down
1. tombs; 2. mint; 3. code; 4. urns; 5. evidence; 6. Herculaneum; 8. Egyptian; 9. year; 13. diary; 14. Stone Age; 15. barges; 17. census; 18. Layard; 19. clues; 23. odd; 26. B.C.

Index